WOMEN: The Fifth World

by Elise Boulding

CONTENTS

1	The Invisible World of Women.	3
2	The Price of Civilization	8
3	Women's Alternatives and Reforms, Ancient and Modern	14
4	The Women's Movement Becomes Global.	23
5	The Fifth World Today: Statistics and Realities	34
6	The Future of Women in the Old World of Power.	43
7	The Vision of the Future.	56
	Statistical tables and charts on pp. 22, 24, 25, 37, 39, 40, 41, 44, 45, 46	
	Appendix: List of Women's Organizations.	59
	Talking It Over	61

HEADLINE Series, 248, February 1980 $2.00

Cover design: Design Works

The Author

ELISE BOULDING heads the sociology department at Dartmouth College. She was born in Norway and received her formal education in the United States, including a Ph.D. degree from the University of Michigan. She taught at the University of Colorado (1967–78), has undertaken numerous studies on conflict and peace, development, family life, and women in society, and is a member of the United States Commission for UNESCO. Among her published works on the status of women is *The Underside of History: A View of Women through Time,* on which she has drawn for some of the material in the present essay.

The Foreign Policy Association

The Foreign Policy Association is a private, nonprofit, nonpartisan educational organization. Its purpose is to stimulate wider interest and more effective participation in, and greater understanding of, world affairs among American citizens. Among its activities is the continuous publication, dating from 1935, of the HEADLINE Series pamphlets. The authors of these pamphlets are responsible for factual accuracy and for the views expressed. FPA itself takes no position on issues of United States foreign policy.

Editorial Advisory Committee
Hans J. Morgenthau, *chairman*

W. Phillips Davison   William H. McNeill
Keith Goldhammer   Edwin Newman
Antonie T. Knoppers   Richard H. Ullman

The HEADLINE Series (ISSN 0017-8780) is published February, April, August, October and December by the Foreign Policy Association, Inc., 205 Lexington Ave., New York, N.Y. 10016. Chairman, Carter L. Burgess; Editor, Wallace Irwin, Jr.; Associate Editor, Gwen Crowe. Subscription rates, $8.00 for 5 issues; $15.00 for 10 issues; $21.00 for 15 issues. Single copy price $2.00. Discount 25% on 10 to 99 copies; 30% on 100 to 499; 35% on 500 to 999; 40% on 1,000 or more. Payment must accompany order for $5 or less. Second-class postage paid at New York, N.Y. Copyright 1980 by Foreign Policy Association, Inc. Composed and printed at Science Press, Ephrata, Penn.

Library of Congress Catalog No. 80-65602
ISBN 0-87124-059-9

1
The Invisible World of Women

Our subject in this essay is the place of women in the modern world—what it is and what it might become. It is a brief look at a very long story. It is addressed not only to women and those who are primarily concerned with women's rights and the women's movement, but to whoever cares about the human quality of the world community of today and of the future. For the sufferings and perils of humanity in our time cannot be relieved unless the predicament of the female half of the human race is perceived and understood far better than has been the case up to the present. As that awareness and understanding increase, not one half but both halves of the people of the world cannot fail to benefit.

This is one of several issues of the HEADLINE Series, dealing with international topics of special humanistic significance, whose publication over the years 1978-80 is being assisted by the National Endowment for the Humanities.

Let us begin the story at the United Nations—an institution which, like our subject, is global in extent and modern in its outlook. As the year 1970 approached, the UN was rounding out its first quarter-century. Its member governments, representing most of the peoples of the world, had plenty to worry and argue about together, and, as usual, it was wars and political crises that dominated the headlines. The members had also become increasingly worried about the underlying conditions, especially the economic conditions, that in great measure caused the crises.

One of the basic aims expressed in the UN Charter is "to achieve international cooperation in solving international problems of an economic, social, cultural, or humanitarian character." As Western colonial empires began to dissolve in the UN's first decade, it had become clear that the greatest need for that kind of cooperation was going to be among the ever more numerous poor nations of what we now call the "third world." Yet by the end of the 1950s it was evident that despite considerable international cooperation, most of the poorer countries were not getting their problems solved at all.

The great idea then emerged of declaring the 1960s a Development Decade. It was to be a time of catching up for all the societies that had been left by the wayside in the 20th-century march of progress. By 1969, however, despite still greater international efforts, very little catching up had taken place in most third-world countries. So the 1970s were declared the Second Development Decade. A few developing countries by then, mostly those richly endowed with oil, were leaping forward into wealth and rapid economic development. But far more still lagged behind. Rural and urban poverty appeared so deep-rooted in large areas that development experts began to speak of a "fourth world" of the desperately poor. In many countries, great wealth and abject poverty were seen side by side.

Why this continuing difficulty in achieving one of the world community's basic aims: an improvement in the economic and social well-being of the poor? The reasons discussed by political leaders and their economic advisers were many and complex; but most of them tended to ignore a small chorus of voices pointing out that *none of the development programs was giving attention to women*. The *fifth world*, that special set of spaces in every society where women carry out their productive roles, was being left out.

The fifth world exists invisibly, uncounted and unassisted, on every continent, in the family farms and kitchen gardens, in the nurseries and kitchens of the planet. The fifth world also sends its fingers out to the most poorly paid work spaces of business, industry, and the service sector. Within the rural and nonindustrialized parts of that fifth world, women give birth to babies, produce milk to feed them, grow food and process it, provide water and fuel, make other goods, build houses, make and repair roads, serve as the beasts of burden that walk the roads and sit in the markets to sell what their hands have made. By ignoring this world of women, so basically involved in human productivity of every kind, development planners were not only perpetrating an injustice on the women themselves by failing to help them improve their conditions of working and living, but they were sabotaging their own development strategies. How was it possible to make such a mistake? How is it possible to continue making it right up to the present?

Development planners have predominantly been Western men, or Western-trained men, imbued with the Western myth that a woman's chief place is in the home, by the side of a man, caring for children with the means he brings to her. This myth has been so persistent that Western development experts have been able to go into third (and the oil-poor fourth) world countries to give development aid without ever noticing the fifth world at all. Yet all the while members of that fifth world, by the hundreds of millions, in addition to their work as mothers and housewives, continue to double (as their mothers and grandmothers have done for centuries) as field hands on the small farms and plantations of the world. With little or no thought for these realities, development planners have laid their main stress on industrialization at the expense of agriculture and rural life, so that farms and villages have been losing more and more of their able-bodied men to the factories and construction sites. This situation has put heavy stress on the women who are left to tend the farm without male help. And to make matters still worse, development experts provide few, if any, simple labor-saving technological innovations that could lighten the farm woman's burdens and make her more economically productive.

The result is that in most parts of the developing world the only source of aid for a farm woman is her children. The producer must breed her own help, and the opportunity to conceive children has become the main economic benefit she derives from her husband, commuting at intervals from his distant job. From this situation, which is painful enough for her, flow still further painful results for the nation as a whole. Farm productivity is breaking down, food production is declining, and the number of babies is going up. In many developing countries which once produced more than enough food for their own peoples, large annual food imports to feed exploding populations—a shockingly high percentage of them young children—have become a dismal necessity.

Such are some of the conditions that have made the development decades a fiasco in so much of the developing third world. No single mistake has contributed more to this massive failure than the inattention of governments and development experts to the role of women in social and economic life.

And what of the condition of women in that world of "developed" countries to which the United States belongs? For all of their highly visible affluence and their periodic strivings toward greater social justice, the nations of the capitalist first world, and of the Marxist second world too, have also lagged in their attention to that seemingly invisible fifth world of women, and have neglected its resources of energy and talent. And these countries, too, pay a heavy human price for their neglect. The problem, then, is universal—partly because of basic defects in the familiar process of development, industrialization, urbanization and modernization. A great deal of rethinking concerning this process seems to be in order, and indeed some of it is well under way.

During the 1960s, mainly because of these shared frustrations with the development process, awareness of the neglected social and economic role of women spread in many nations, developed and developing alike. National governments, male-dominated though they are, became increasingly aware of it through the debates of the UN. The latter's deliberations led to the designation of 1975 as International Women's Year. In June and July of that year the World Conference of International Women's Year was held in Mexico City. Among its actions was the inauguration of a UN Decade for Women, 1975-1985.

Thus the governments of the world, acting through the UN, belatedly recognized how critical women are to economic and social development processes of every kind; and the situation of women as economic producers, bearers of children and weavers of the social fabric was placed at long last on the world agenda.

As this is written, we are approaching the halfway mark in the UN Decade for Women. A follow-up conference in Copenhagen, Denmark is scheduled for July 1980. It is a good time to consider the position of women in world society, past and present—and to think about what all of us, women and men alike, would wish that position to be in the future.

2

The Price of Civilization

The idea that women belong in the home and men in the fields or the shop, *i.e.* that only men are "producers," is neither universal nor very ancient. It has gained widest acceptance in the Western world, mainly as a result of the experiences of urbanization and industrialization in the past couple of hundred years.

What we know of prehistory (and can infer from studying the few stone-age cultures that survived into our century) indicates that, during the hundreds of thousands of years when the human species lived as hunters and gatherers, women, men and children shared the same experience worlds. They traveled together, learned how to scan new terrains together, and on the whole acquired the same skills. Women hunted as well as men, men did food gathering as well as women, and both cared for small children. Some differentiation of sex roles did arise when hunters took off after larger game which might require several days to run down, for nursing and pregnant women were at a disadvantage in long runs, as were small children. But the long runs were infrequent, and male dominance over the group did not develop from them. Roles were still fluid for both sexes.

Once agricultural settlements appeared—by 12,000 B.C. at the latest—the previously slight differentiation of male and female roles received a sharp push toward further development. Women tilled the fields and men went further and further away to hunt, as nearby game became scarcer. The experience worlds of the two sexes began to separate out. It was men who found the water holes, the ocher pits, the flint deposits, the faraway next village. Men began to acquire a higher status from this advantage in access to resources. Women *walked* the trade routes men found, bearing children on their backs and goods to sell on their heads, while men ran on still further to find new trade routes.

It was not that the women were not mobile. As in the earlier nomadic state, they still traveled a lot, carrying children and household goods. But they traveled more encumbered. Even today, in nomadic societies that have survived into the 20th century, men will carry babies and very young children. In settled agricultural societies, only women carry babies and very young children; the men take on parental responsibility only when the offspring are fully ambulatory and partly self-sufficient. It was the sloughing off of additional child care responsibility on women (beyond their biologically determined role of giving birth and suckling) that provided the initial kick to role differentiation. The less time men spent caring for and nurturing children, the more they spent acquiring surplus resources and power and dominance. The beginning of the separation out of women's life and work from the larger social sphere ensued.

The separation was very slow and gradual, however, and only became sharp in urban areas. Even today it is far from being an accomplished fact worldwide. The majority of the human race have been farmers for many thousands of years, and the farming way of life is a partnership. It generates a type of familial division of labor—which leaves separate and autonomous spheres for women and men. There is no universal pattern for the division of labor—what women do in one society men do in another, and both do in a third. Often a husband and wife will each have separate plots of land and separate craft and trading enterprises. The autonomous spheres principle, with each spouse retaining control of her or his own profits, and giving and receiving financial credit separately, is very widespread.

This conclusion is borne out by many studies of preindustrial societies of the 20th century. In such societies women are typically engaged not only in farming and craft work but also in trade, handling of money, credit transactions, savings, and investment. In none of these societies do women fail to accumulate and invest capital, whether in the form of land, livestock, gold, or other commodities. Some of the capital is in the form of dowry, or bride-price. While a woman does not necessarily have control over all of the bridal fund, in no case is she left without the possibility of accumulating capital over which she will have exclusive control. The nomadic Fulani of West Africa, for example, distinguish between cattle owned jointly by husband and wife, and cattle owned exclusively by the woman. Women have their own cash income from trade in cattle and dairy products, and all ownership of clothes, tools and furniture is separate for husbands and wives. The dowry, which "belongs" to the wife and is "cared for" by the husband, is considered as the children's inheritance, an item separate from her private capital.

In some New Guinea societies money flows with the movements of women between groups. "Women are like trade stores," and "Women walk about and bring plenty of valuables" are revealing folk sayings. Interestingly, though the men regard themselves as the decision-makers and the controllers of all the significant transactions in the society, with the women as their servant-producers, the women think of themselves as independent transactors.

Women may lose their rights as preindustrial societies "develop" into modern states. Black women in South Africa cannot now legally assert the inheritance rights they had under tribal law, yet, according to author H.J. Simons, "many thousands of widows officiate in practice as the heads of their households." In this case the old law has proved stronger than the new.

Who legally *owns* the land, however, is of minimal importance in many of these societies, since rights to the *use* of land are assigned by the tribe or extended family. On the other hand, the rights of women to independent accumulation of goods, livestock, etc. are very important. Surpluses are carefully "invested" by women in order to pass on as large an inheritance as possible to daughters (sometimes also to sons). The women of an extended family are a type of female credit association, enabling members to finance new ventures such as the acquisition of new livestock, jewelry, etc.

The City and the New Division of Labor

For better or worse, these preindustrial agricultural societies, in which women and men hold approximately equal status, are fast disappearing from the face of the earth. Their disappearance began many centuries ago with the introduction of cash cropping to feed the growing cities and manufacturing centers which cannot feed themselves. This new division of labor led to great increases in productivity. But for this gain a heavy price was paid, mainly by women. Invariably, as Ester Boserup has shown in her book *Women's Role in Economic Development,* the intrusion of cash cropping into the life of the farm disrupts the family production partnership and leads to male dominance. The industrialized countries passed through this phase centuries ago, reorganizing production into a predominantly male sphere with auxiliary roles available to women only if they left the homestead and entered the factory at low wages. Even earlier, the urban migration in Europe had detached women from their rural means of production. They lived resourceless in urban tenements with children to raise and, all too often, no means of feeding them. There are few kitchen gardens in city tenements. A husband, if present (many women migrants to the city had children but no spouse), rarely earned enough to support the whole family.

For a great proportion of city dwellers of both sexes, the city has never been kind. But all through history it has borne down with unequal weight on women, widening the inequality of roles and status between the sexes. This was not uniformly true at all social levels, to be sure. At the bottom, for the very poor, the unskilled workers and most slaves, squalor and suffering were the common lot of women and men. At the top, on the other hand, women shared significantly, though by no means equally, in the power of the rulers and their control over resources. The aristocratic matron—from ancient Mesopotamia and Egypt right up to the industrial revolution in Europe—typically administered a country estate as well as a household in the city, farming and trading on a considerable scale and displaying a high order of executive skill.

It is especially in what today is called the middle class—the families of merchants, scribes, petty functionaries and administrators, few in number at first but growing more numerous over the centuries—that role differentiation at the expense of women has been most evident. From 2000 B.C. to the present, boys in such families were educated and sent out into the world while girls were not. Thus there evolved the fully privatized role of the urban middle-class wife, the "full-time homemaker." Eventually, even for the aristocracy, as Europe's landed estates began to disappear in the age of industrialization, women of that most privileged class became confined in the homemaker role along with their middle-class sisters.

Also increasingly disadvantaged over time have been the women of the skilled-worker or artisan class. In the ancient cities of Greece and Rome, women labored in small textile and craft workshops, ran the corner bakery and brewery, and provided the middle and upper classes with domestic, health and beauty services. In the early craft guilds of medieval Europe, although women had far from equal status and training opportunities, they did have the advantage of a workplace which was also a home, so that domestic and workshop functions could be flexibly combined. But two conditions have operated against skilled women workers. One, which began in 14th-century Europe and culminated in the industrial revolution, was the gradual enlargement of the craft workshops until some of them employed thousands of workers, principally unskilled workers with no rights in the guild. Thus there gradually evolved the modern factory, usually located a long way from home. This was a big step backward for women with children, since adequate facilities for daytime child care usually did not exist—and still do not exist today. This was an age when it became common for mothers to carry their babies to the factory, drugged to keep them quiet; or to put them in "baby farms" where mortality was high; or to resort to infanticide.

The other adverse condition is of ancient date: the low wages paid to women on the fictitious ground that their need is less since, supposedly, they all live in households headed by a male breadwinner. That this male-head-of-household fiction has persisted so long is amazing. The truth is that in any setting, urban or rural, in any period of history for which data are available, one-fifth to one-half of the heads of households were women. (The current world figure is 38 percent.) Many of these women were rearing children without male partners because of widowhood, desertion, divorce, or because—as in some African countries even today—they were plural wives infrequently visited by the husband with full responsibility for the care and feeding of their children. They may have been never-married women driven by poverty to sell sexual services, raising children with minimal resources. They may have been not-yet-married women who would later assume domestic roles, or never-married women who chose an independent way of life as entertainers, intellectuals, or merchants (and were often erroneously labeled by historians as hetaerae, courtesans, or prostitutes). They might or might not have chosen to raise children of their own. Most of them, except for the wealthy and the independent entrepreneurs, had to struggle to make ends meet. They had to accept the low wages established through the fiction of male support—and, in many times and places, through the reality of competition with slave labor.

3
Women's Alternatives and Reforms, Ancient and Modern

It is probable that from the earliest beginning of the differentiation of roles that began ages ago to close in on woman, relegating her to a narrower and more subordinate role as wife/mother in a male-headed household, there were women who devised more satisfying alternatives. We know that such alternatives have existed during the entire period from about 500 B.C. to the industrial revolution. And after that great historical divide came, further constricting women's lives, new and widespread reform efforts began which eventually became the women's movement of today. In this chapter we recall a few highlights of the story especially as it developed in the Western world.

Alternatives in Antiquity and the Middle Ages

One alternative was celibacy. The nun role has existed from early times in Hinduism, in Buddhism and, finally, in Christianity and Islam. Although religious orders for women took different forms in Asia, the Middle East and Europe, some religious alternatives for women that did not involve bearing and raising children were present in all these societies. Between A.D. 500 and 1400 there was an extraordinary flowering of convent culture in Europe. This culture produced science, art and literature, and a social service infrastructure in the fields of health, education and welfare unparalleled until the 19th century. While nuns paid a price in celibacy and in their isolation, living in protected niches within the male-dominated structure of the Catholic Church, there is abundant evidence that they found true freedom in their chosen life. The achievements of nuns of the Benedictine and Cistercian orders, and of outstanding women like St. Hildegarde in Germany (1098-1178) and St. Birgitta in Sweden (1303-73) ranged from the organization of manufacturing enterprises on a considerable scale to the production of important intellectual works, the composition of music and poetry, service to the poor and, occasionally, influential intervention in politics. These women religious made creative use of their freedom. There was joy in convent life in those centuries, as well as before and since. The 19th and 20th centuries have seen a second explosion of creativity through celibacy, partly within religious orders and partly outside of them. Today there are approximately 2 million nuns in the world, coming from all the major religious traditions.

In addition to celibacy in the convent, there was the *béguinage*—a type of urban commune, religious in inspiration but outside the Church. It enlisted rural women or béguines, who had come to the city during the migrations of the 1200s and 1300s. Invented by women, the béguinages were so successful as craft workshops that they were seen as serious threats to some of the male-dominated craft guilds and were persecuted by guild folk. Many of them also incurred the wrath of the Church by developing a flourishing and largely independent religious life of their own.

Besides the béguines there were also hermitesses—women solitaries who lived in huts by bridges, on the edges of towns, and in forest solitudes all over England and, to a lesser extent, in the rest of Europe. These were a special class of independents in the Middle Ages, able to support themselves through their knowledge of human nature and folk medicine. Since they had little institutional protection of any kind, many of them were burned as witches. Last, there were the vagabonds, the hardworking, fun-loving women who moved partnerless through the Middle Ages, always able to pick up the pennies they needed at a fair or celebration of some kind. When they were willing to settle in a town, they were not infrequently supported by town councils, glad to have resident entertainers for their community. Besides being entertainers, they ran the soup kitchens and the first-aid stations in wars, including the Crusades. They were good soldiers when they were needed as fighters. Altogether, they were a social category for which we have no labels today, and marriage was not on their agenda.

The End of an Era

During the late 1500s and 1600s many of the phenomena described above began to disappear. The craftswomen, the celibates and the vagabonds all declined in numbers and status. In the guilds in particular there was a rapid loss of rights and status for women. Men were feeling the pressure of women as competitors in the labor market and successfully pressed for their expulsion from guild after guild. This transition era initiated the prolonged suffering of both rural and urban female laborers as they were squeezed out of secure medieval work statuses. The hermitess or vagabond of the 14th century became the work-deadened automaton of the 17th and 18th centuries. Rural laboring women went hungry, and the children of women in the factories were rounded up like cattle and placed in workhouses or shipped overseas to labor in the colonies. Married and single women alike were trapped by the formulas of "supplemental" pittance wages for women.

This was also the period when the gentlewoman in straitened circumstances appeared—the middle-class woman without husband, and without training and resources, who could not enter domestic service because of her social status. She became a governess or a companion in homes of slightly better off middle-class people, working for little more than bread and board, often in a position close to that of the household slave of Greek and Roman times. Just below her in station was the domestic, even more of a household slave. By the 1700s, these women began to emigrate overseas to new hardships, but also to new opportunities.

It was the 19th century that witnessed the emergence of new social-economic doctrines calling, among other things, for a basic reform of the situation of women. Women and men alike, whether Saint-Simonians, anarchist socialists, or Marxist socialists, all saw the necessity for society to free women from entrapment in the role of mere bearers and feeders of children and providers of domestic maintenance for everyone. However, none of the reformers looked back to the time when men had shared some of these duties with women. In their plans, every domestic function except biological childbearing was to be taken over by the state.

Since no socialist state could afford to implement such plans, and no capitalist state wanted to—and few men were interested in sharing the burden—it was easy to turn it back to women in the end. The famous "return to matriarchy" movement has to be seen in that context. Led by Ellen Key of Sweden around the turn of this century, it sought to restore full legal head-of-household rights to women independently of marital status. In Key's view, women could carry out their traditional child-rearing roles *better* if they were freed from dependence on men! In spite of appearances to the contrary, most of the 19th-century utopian movements from Brook Farm to New Harmony left women's traditional roles unchanged. Only the Shakers and the Mormons offered something different: the former the freedom of celibacy, the latter the freedom of having co-wives with whom to share farm labor. Both sects attracted women in droves.

Women's New Internationalism

As the industrial revolution progressed, the hitherto small group of underemployed middle-class urban women in Europe and North America expanded rapidly—and a new view of the world took shape for many of them. About 150 years ago such women rather quickly shifted from an attitude of open-mouthed wonder about far-away places to a comprehension of continents linked not only by the benefits of normal commerce but by the evils of the slave trade, economic oppression and imperial war. While statesmen and revolutionaries were locked in struggles over national independence, while merchants mined Africa for black human gold, and while colonies staked out territorial and commercial claims in the name of God and king, these women were feeling the pull of quite a different current. This other current was internationalism, which might be thought of as the undertow of nationalism and imperialist expansion. It pulled them in the opposite direction from most of society. Not only women, of course, felt this undertow. But because even the most imaginative of men were accustomed to leadership roles, and did not know how to accept women as collaborators, many of the women who felt it were driven to seek each other out and form their own groups.

In this way a new phenomenon appeared in the history of women—a vast increase in the scale and complexity of their concerns. Women had played a role for centuries as advocates of justice and of the more equitable distribution of society's goods, but almost entirely on the local or, at most, national level. Now, whether they were concerned with slavery, economic oppression of workers, or wars of conquest, they were beginning to think in terms of global rather than national welfare.

This new internationalism received a major stimulus as women participated in the series of international fairs that helped to build the infrastructure of the new world community between 1851 and 1893. The first international exposition was held in London in 1851, and it was followed by expositions in Paris and other cities in the next decades. In 1893 at the Chicago Exposition, a congress of women was formally organized for the first time. The papers presented at the congress give an overview of how the older "lady of the manor house" style of service, in both England and America, was translated into modern approaches to social needs. Baroness Angela Georgina Burdett-Coutts of England, who presented a report to the congress on the philanthropic work of English women, herself embodied the transition between the old aristocracy and the new middle-class women. Many of the innovations in education and welfare services and home services for working women and children, for prisoners and for migrants, which were developed and reported at about that time, have yet to be generally adopted by any society.

Peace and labor reform were among the early causes for which women organized. In the 1820s and 1830s, the first all-women national peace societies were founded in England and America, and by 1852 the Olive Leaf Circles were issuing the first international women's publication, *Sisterly Voices*. In 1840 the French-Peruvian Flora Tristan Moscosa traveled around the world promoting her plan for a worldwide workers' international, later spelled out in her book, *L'Union Ouvrière* (1843). The first *La Voix des Femmes,* predecessor of the Canadian peace organization of that name formed in the 1960's, was born as a socialist paper in Paris in the 1840s.

By the time of the establishment of the short-lived Paris Commune in 1871 many women had apprenticed themselves to the new internationalism. When Louise Michel broke into the bakeries of Lyon in 1882 to redistribute bread to the poor, she was not just imitating the housewives who had rioted for bread as a purely local issue at different times and places in the Europe of the 1700s; she was inspired by the new socialist-anarchist vision of postimperial society transcending national borders. By the 1880s and 1890s, the vision of an international socialist community based on nonviolence and the repudiation of nationalism was being articulated by Clara Zetkin and Rosa Luxemburg. These two women were only the most visible members of a large sisterhood that determinedly fought the nationalist chauvinism of the majority of their male colleagues in the socialist movement. They fought, and lost, but their influence survived them. Religious and socialist visions intertwined in the work of women like Elise van Calcar of the Netherlands, Annie Besant of England and Olive Schreiner of South Africa.

Groups of women sprang up all over Europe throughout the second half of the 19th century, women moving to a different rhythm than that of the military drumbeats then being heard everywhere. Among their leaders were Concepción Arenal in

Spain; Fredrika Bremer, Rosalie Olivercrona and the controversial Ellen Key, all in Sweden; and Beatrice Webb and Octavia Hill in England. Fredrika Bremer was the first to propose an international association of women for peace. Priscilla Peckover, an English Quaker, built up an international network of women with members in France, the Rhineland, Hanover, Rome, Warsaw, Constantinople, Russia, Japan, Polynesia, Portugal and the United States.

Austrian Bertha von Suttner, author of one of the century's major works on disarmament, *Die Waffen nieder* (Down with Arms) which appeared in 1889, and was translated into English in 1892, persuaded Alfred Nobel to found the Nobel Peace Prize. During World War I Jane Addams of the United States helped convene at the Hague a group of women whose husbands were fighting each other at Europe's battlefronts. This group would continue under the name of the Women's International League for Peace and Freedom, and would contribute to both the moral conscience and the scholarly knowhow that focused on the effort to create alternative institutions to war as an instrument of national diplomacy. Frances Willard, an American who founded the Woman's Christian Temperance Union, was an eloquent spokesperson for the new world view of women. E.P. Gordon, in her book about the WCTU, quotes these words of Willard's:

We are a world republic of women—without distinction of race or

Jane Addams (1860–1935) gained world recognition as a founder of Chicago's Hull-House, a pioneering center in social work among the urban poor. She later joined the peace movement, headed the Women's International League for Peace and Freedom and was a co-winner of the Nobel Peace Prize.

The Bettman Archive, Inc.

> color—who recognize no sectarianism in politics, no sex in citizenship. Each of us is as much a part of the world's union as is any other woman; it is our great, growing, beautiful home....

As these examples show, the new internationalism was not just an extension of women's older concerns—with their own status in family and society—to the world scale. Something else was going on—a rethinking of social structures and social roles. Women were beginning to recognize their own complicity in war and injustice, for these would be easier for men to perpetuate as long as women accepted their traditional underside nurturing roles. So war, slavery, economic injustice and the misery of the urban poor all appeared on their agenda, an intricate complex of issues. Even the Florence Nightingales became politicized, and men fought against new civic roles for women because they feared the changes that would follow. The women's rights movement developed almost incidentally out of this situation, as women found civic problem-solving roles closed to them because of their sex.

Between 1880 and 1900 five transnational women's organizations were born. Two of them were religious in orientation, the World Young Women's Christian Association (WYWCA) and the World Women's Christian Temperance Union (WWCTU); one was professional, the International Council of Nurses (ICN); and two were cultural, the General Federation of Women's Clubs (GFWC) and the International Council of Women (ICW). In each case they began as local women's organizations in one country, but quickly spread elsewhere because of women's high level of readiness to enter into transnational community.

Women were also entering other transnational organizations and working alongside men during this same period, but since men showed a persistent unwillingness to accept women as full collaborators in the mixed organizations, all-women's organizations continued to grow and multiply. The most activist separate women's groups in this early period were the YWCA and WCTU. Urban-based, these groups had a strong commitment to the problems of the young working woman combating alcoholism and rape, and of the deserted, widowed, or single woman with children—problems encountered in every country. They combined an instinct for practical community problem-solving with a powerful aspiration toward a kind of moral purity and spiritual welfare that does not translate easily into the late 20th-century vocabulary.

The next era of growth of women's international organizations came in the years 1900 to 1915. Five more religious organizations were born in this period, and the first three international relations associations.

For increasing numbers of women in many countries, it became clear that their concerns with peace, justice and social progress depended on political as well as on private decisions, and hence had a political corollary: the right of women to vote. In England the first appeal for votes for women was published in 1825. In the United States the women's suffrage movement was launched in 1848 by women leaders in the antislavery movement. But it took generations of organized effort, ranging from sweet reason to life-risking militancy, before male resistance to extending the franchise to women began to crumble in the English-speaking world and in Europe in the decades before and just after World War I. Today the right of women to vote is virtually universal. (See Table 1.)

Table 1: Women's Suffrage

Year	Number of countries where men and women could vote in national elections on equal terms
1900	1
1910	3
1920	15
1930	21
1940	30
1950	69
1960	92
1970	127
1975	129

From: Kathleen Newland, *The Sisterhood of Man*. New York, W.W. Norton & Company, 1979. With permission.

4
The Women's Movement Becomes Global

The women's movement at the outset of World War I was largely confined to the countries of its origin in Europe and North America. Even in these countries the feminist consciousness receded during the two great wars, when women as well as men threw themselves into the war effort. And it receded even further in the boom years that followed World War II, especially in the United States, where it faded into the "back to the home" movement so graphically described by Betty Friedan in her classic book, *The Feminine Mystique*.

The back-to-the-home movement, however, was in part only a literary fiction. What really happened was that more and more women entered the work force while still carrying their traditional domestic burdens. Participation in the U.S. labor force by women with children under the age of six climbed steadily in the period 1948–67. During the same period the number of places in day care centers steadily declined. (See Figures 1 and 2.) Clearly, authorities were responding to the fiction of mothers at home rather than to the fact of mothers working. The situation was

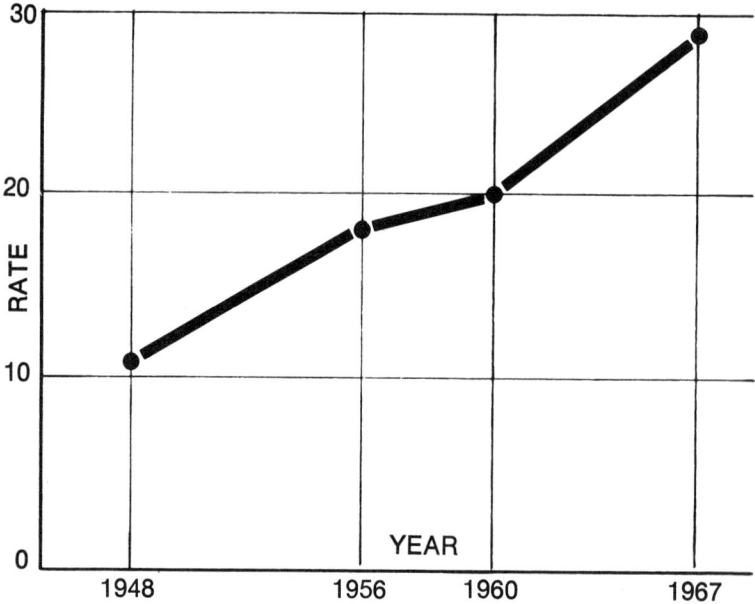

Figure 1: Percent of mothers with children under age 6 who were in the U.S. labor force, 1948, 1956, 1960 and 1967.

Source for Figures 1 & 2: Elise Boulding, joint with Patricia Boston Trainer, "Quality of Life, U.S.A.: Costs and Benefits of Urbanization and Industrialization, 1900-1970." Conference Proceedings, 2nd Annual Sess., Institute of Environmental Awareness, San Diego, Calif., April 27, 1971.

aggravated by a massive internal migration of poor Americans, both black and white, from southern farms to northern cities. The predicament of poor families headed by working mothers soon became—and still remains—one of the paramount social problems facing the women's movement in the United States and elsewhere in the industrialized world.

Spurred by such domestic issues—as well as by anxiety over international tensions arising from the war in Vietnam and the nuclear arms race—by the mid-1960s the feminist consciousness in the Western world was undergoing a rebirth both domestically and at the international level.

Figure 2: Number of Children Cared for in Day Care Centers, 1947 and 1965.

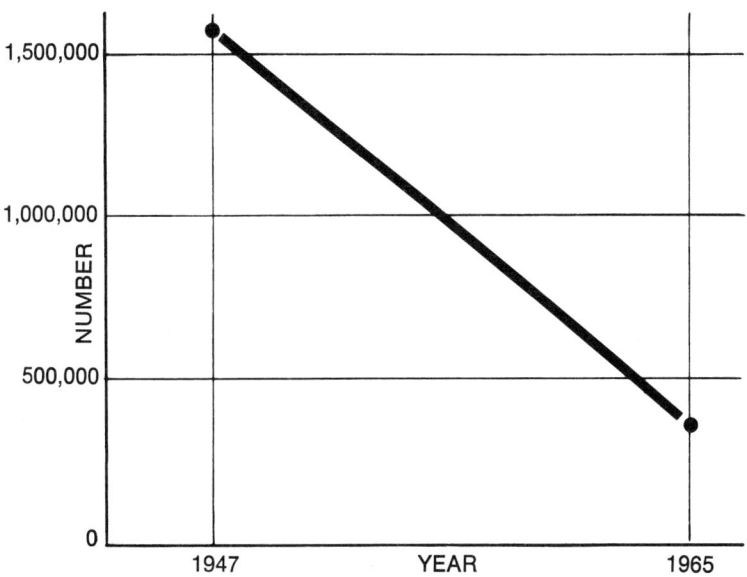

The Meeting of North and South

Almost simultaneously, the women's movement was being extended far beyond the Western community and achieving a truly global reach.

The first encounters of the Western women's movement with women of Asia and Africa—what would much later be called the third world—occurred in the 19th century. Many contacts at that time were at the elite level—wives of diplomats and businessmen working with their counterparts in such capitals as Peking, Bangkok, New Delhi and Lagos. There were also the rank-and-file contacts of missionary-trained women representing organizations like the YWCA and the WCTU, and endeavoring according to the views and concepts of that time to improve the condition of women in the countries to which they were assigned. All these were Western initiatives, and thus essentially one-sided, in a world where colonialism was still the order of the day. But they were a beginning.

Only in the present generation, when decolonization has at last released people of the third world to speak with their own voices and out of their own cultural experience, has the women's movement begun to become truly worldwide both in its membership and in its perceptions. Western women have begun to listen to these other voices, and to learn that in every continent there is a history not only of the oppression and segregation of women through purdah and similar practices, but also of the *emergence* of women, working in and for society and walking freely in the public spaces of their cultures as merchants, managers, professionals, saints, reformers, revolutionaries. As we noted in Chapter 1, the fundamental criticism of past concepts of economic development, heard at the UN in recent years, arose partly because women of the third world were at last being noticed and listened to.

How International Women's Year Evolved

Gradually these tensions experienced by women, both in the Western world and in the third world, brought women's awareness to a new peak. The women's transnational associations formed during earlier periods of feminist awareness were ready and waiting when the new women's movement came to life.

Appropriately, the setting for this global stage of the women's movement was the UN. Its commissions on the status of women and on social development had been laboring in relative obscurity for decades, producing important but little-noted studies and recommendations on social policy. But never yet had the basic issues of woman's place in society caught the full attention of national leaders. The time for that was now approaching.

An important step occurred when the UN General Assembly proclaimed 1965 as International Cooperation Year (ICY). The original proposal had come from Jawaharlal Nehru, India's prime minister, on a visit to the UN four years earlier. But the impulse came in great part from the kitchen of a Kansas housewife who conceived the idea, one day as she was doing her household chores, that the UN might declare a year in which ordinary women and men everywhere could help to build a community through small cooperative projects. She offered her suggestion to a friend who happened just then to be conferring with India's UN delegates on initiatives their prime minister might propose in his UN address. The idea was adopted and, backed by Nehru's prestige, the International Cooperation Year sailed through the Assembly. An international women's network quickly sprang into being to organize projects for the year in many countries.

Between the women's inexperience and the international bureaucracy's inertia, the ICY fell short of its sponsors' ambitious hopes, but for the international community of women it proved to be the start of a long and constructive chain of events. The women who traveled together in teams during 1964 to prepare the ICY did not disappear back into their kitchens. They were present in 1972 at the UN Conference on the Human Environment in Stockholm; in 1974 at the World Population Conference in Bucharest and the World Food Conference in Rome. They attended the annual sessions of the Committee on Disarmament in Geneva. Each time they came in larger numbers, and with better documentation to show how the conference subject impinged on women. Each time they also saw how blind most of their male colleagues were to the importance of women's roles in economic production and social welfare. This was the more discouraging because governments appointed so few women as delegates to most international conferences. Most of the women, no matter how much expert knowledge they had, stood on the outside at these conferences as petitioners and protesters. The idea for International Women's Year was born out of this mounting frustration on the part of women of the international community so much of whose knowledge and wisdom was not being listened to.

It was an important turning point. For the first time, women attained the influence needed to raise the issues of women's rights and status from the valiant but obscure Commission on the Status of Women and other bodies to which the UN had relegated them for many years, and to make them an important focus of attention for the UN's male-dominated member governments—to say nothing of its male-dominated Secretariat. It took years of work, including the drafting of a "Declaration of the Elimination of Discrimination Against Women," adopted by the General Assembly in 1967; a program of action to implement that declaration, adopted in 1970; and in 1972, building on these previous actions, approval by the Assembly of a proposal to declare 1975 as International Women's Year, with its primary aim "to promote equality between men and women."

The Mexico City conference in June and July 1975, which climaxed International Women's Year, was the first high-level UN conference at which the majority of delegations from the governments of the world were headed by women. This alone was a symbolic victory. Still more important, although many of the delegates were men, often displaying little knowledge of the situation of women, it was mainly women of the international women's movement who led in the preparations for, and determined the results of, the Mexico conference. Some came as official delegates, others as representatives of nongovernmental organizations (NGOs). The latter were present in strength at the conference. Some 6,000 women from all over the world attended a nongovernmental forum known as the IWY Tribune. For most of those present it was the first opportunity for an exchange of views and experiences between Western feminists and their counterparts in the third world.

A World Plan of Action

The main product of all these efforts took the form of a World Plan of Action, approved by the conference and subsequently by the UN General Assembly. It is perhaps the most significant and far-reaching public document ever written about the participation of women in society. It spells out the relationships between the situation of women in each country and the global problems of inequality, maldevelopment and war. It makes explicit the need to keep women in mind whenever social progress is under discussion. It has ushered in a new era of awareness on the part of governments of the importance of that 51 percent of their citizenry who are women. And to inaugurate this new era it has designated the years 1975-1985 as the UN Decade for Women.

The introduction to the World Plan of Action strikes the keynote for the whole document and deserves to be quoted at length. It begins by reminding governments of their repeated declarations in various previous UN documents that the full and complete development of a country, the welfare of the world and the cause of peace require the maximum participation of women as well as men in all fields. It goes on to state:

> Despite these solemn pronouncements and notwithstanding the work accomplished in particular by the UN Commission on the Status of Women and the specialized agencies concerned, progress in translating these principles into practical reality is proving slow and uneven.
>
> There are significant differences in the status of women in different countries and regions of the world which are rooted in the political, economic and social structure, the cultural framework and the level of development of each country, and in the social category of women within a given country. However, basic similarities unite women of all countries, the most notable being the persisting *de facto* gap between the economic and social status of women and that of men.
>
> As a result of the uneven development which prevails in international economic relations, three-quarters of humanity is faced with urgent and pressing social and economic problems. The women among them are even more affected by such problems, and improvements in their situation must be an integral part of the global project for the establishment of a new economic order....
>
> The achievement of equality between men and women implies that they should have equal rights, opportunities and responsibilities to enable them to develop their talents and capabilities for their own personal fulfillment and the benefit of society. To that end, a reassessment of the functions and roles traditionally allotted to each sex within the family and the community at large is essential. The necessity of a change in the traditional role of men

as well as of women must be recognized. In order to allow for women's equal participation in all societal activities, men must accept shared responsibility for home and children. The objective is not to give women a preferential role, but to ensure the complete assimilation of men and women in the social order. . . .

International cooperation and peace requires national independence and liberation, the elimination of colonialism and neocolonialism, foreign occupation and *apartheid,* and racial discrimination in all its forms as well as recognition of the dignity of the individual and appreciation of the human person and his or her self-determination. To this end, the plan calls for the full participation of women in all efforts to promote and maintain peace.

It is the aim of the plan to ensure that the original and multidimensional contribution—both actual and potential—of women is not overlooked in existing concepts for development and an improved world economic equilibrium. . . .

The plan itself consists of guidelines for national action for the decade 1975-1985, including:

—the involvement of women in the strengthening of international security and peace through participation at all relevant levels in national, intergovernmental and UN bodies;

—furthering the political participation of women in national societies at every level;

—strengthening educational and training programs for women;

—integrating women workers into the labor force of every country at every level, according to accepted international standards;

—more equitably distributing health and nutrition services to take account of the responsibilities of women everywhere for the health and feeding of their families;

—increasing governmental assistance for the family unit;

—directly involving women, as the primary producers of population, in the development of population programs and other programs affecting the quality of life of individuals of all ages, in family groups and outside them, including housing and social services of every kind.

It is a strong document, both in its assessment of the world situation of women and in the guidelines it lays down—so specific that no government can complain that it does not know where to begin. Moreover, the plan includes a recommendation that each government establish a timetable for achieving specific objectives to implement the guidelines over the five years 1975-80, the first half of the UN Decade for Women.

A Five-Year Assessment

Just how well have governments and international agencies fulfilled the responsibilities they assumed at Mexico City? This is to be a main question for discussion at the mid-decade World Conference of the UN Decade for Women to be held in Copenhagen in July 1980—a session that was in preparation as these pages went to press. Voluminous documentation for the conference has begun to show where progress has been made and where it has not. Some small but significant steps can be recorded:

▶ A Voluntary Fund for the UN Decade for Women has been in operation since shortly after the Mexico City conference. With a mere $9 million in contributions (over half from the United States), by 1979 it had generated over 120 small projects in developing countries aimed at increasing the skills and participation of women in development, especially in agriculture and small-scale rural or village industry, community development, health, nutrition, day care for children, etc. The extent of the influence of such a small program on such a massive global problem remains to be seen, but it is working on the right problems and its approach is imaginative.

▶ Another small step was taken with the establishment by the UN in 1979 of an International Research and Training Institute for the Advancement of Women. It is to be located in the Dominican Republic and has a modest initial funding of $1.8 million.

▶ An international convention to outlaw discrimination against women was adopted by the UN General Assembly in 1979. Although unenforceable internationally, such a convention can be of great value as the first internationally accepted standard of women's rights and status in political life, the courts, education, employment, property ownership, marriage and other aspects of modern life.

▶ The agencies of the UN system, notably the World Bank, UNESCO, the International Labor Organization (ILO), the World Health Organization and the Food and Agriculture Organization, have been increasing their programs aimed specifically at the needs of women in developing countries.

▶ Even in the UN's own profession, diplomacy, there are modest signs of improvement. Seventeen countries, including the United States, reported in 1979 that the percentage of women in their diplomatic services, foreign ministries and delegations to UN conferences had increased since 1975—although in most cases the percentages were still pitifully low.

Turning from the international to the national realm, some fragmentary indication of the progress of women, or lack of it, could be gleaned from national reports prepared for the Copenhagen conference by 73 governments (not quite half the UN membership) on the condition of women in their countries and what steps they were taking to improve matters. With commendable candor, many of the reports bear out the unhappy truth we have reviewed in these pages—how harshly large-scale industrial-urban development has dealt with women, both in the so-called developed countries and in the third world. They also, however, identify small advances here and there—an "affirmative action" policy adopted by the government of Kenya to increase job opportunities for women; opening of vocational education to girls in Greece; special education for pregnant teenagers in Jamaica; a dramatic rise in many countries in the accessibility of birth control technology for women; stronger laws in Europe and North America requiring equal pay for equal work.

Is the glass half full or half empty? Many reporting governments are forthright in their assessment. In developed countries, says a UN analysis of the national reports, the main obstacle to women's equality in education, especially at higher and technical levels, is "the still extremely strong general prejudice within society as a whole," including parents, teachers and guidance counselors. In most developing countries, the story is similar: the poor status of women in the job market is ascribed frankly to "broad societal prejudices" and to "the fact that policy-makers and planners themselves still did not consider the problem to be urgent." Clearly, the instruments for implementation of the Mexico City plan of action are weak, and the motivation of most government officials to implement it is weaker still.

This weakness cannot be laid to mere ill will on the part of officials and administrators. Rather, it seems to be rooted in an historical paradox. On the one hand, government leaders are constantly preoccupied with the world crises of war, hunger and resource depletion, and look upon demands for attention to women's problems as a distraction from this serious business. Yet at the very same historical moment, it has become clear that these crises cannot be resolved without integrating the hitherto excluded female half of the world's population into the problem-solving process. It is as if the tremendous fears and anxieties engendered by the multiple crises of today's world render most decision-makers unable to open their minds to the new concepts and the new data concerning social realities in today's world, and the place of women in it, which are necessary to the solutions they so anxiously seek. Once again we see a demonstration of the psychological truth that a situation of intense threat is the worst possible condition under which to learn something new. Fear rigidifies people, narrows their behavioral repertoire and drives them back to old, "tried and true" ways—even when these ways have ceased to work.

5
The Fifth World Today: Statistics and Realities

Clearly, the nations of the world have a long way to go before they are free of their chronic injustice to women and their consequent injustice to society as a whole. Before we can progress, however, we must know more precisely where we stand today. In this chapter we will look at some key facts and figures about the status of the fifth world of women. Where do women stand in countries at all stages of economic development, from the opulent first world to the poverty-stricken fourth?

The Statistical Gap

One important way in which to gain an understanding of any large-scale social reality is through statistics. For statistics on the status of women, we look primarily to those that are collected by national governments and forwarded to UN statistical offices about the number of women in the labor force, what occupations they are in, what salaries they receive, how much schooling they have completed, how many are illiterate, and (more irregularly reported) how many elective and appointive offices they hold. Information is also collected about their marital status and the numbers of children born to them.

In the wake of the Mexico City conference, an effort has been made in the UN to improve the available statistics on women. Still, however, the material received by the UN from governments is often depressingly thin or absent altogether. A master table compiled by the Secretariat for the 1980 conference shows fairly complete figures on how many females in different age groups there are in each country; somewhat spotty figures on female school enrollment; and, when it comes to illiteracy rates among women and employment of women in the urban sector, there are more blanks than numbers.

Even where numbers are given, we face several kinds of difficulty in interpreting them. To begin with, one of the major problems of women in a male-dominated economy is their invisibility. They are frequently invisible to the census enumerators who count employed persons because much of their productive labor takes place in what we have called the fifth world: the world of the kitchen, the kitchen garden, and the nursery. Economists do not assign a market value to this labor, but use a category called "not economically active homemaker" to cover women in this type of occupation. A second, more elusive category is that of "*other* not economically active women": students, pensioners and "others." A third category of women's labor, hard to pin down, is that of the "unpaid family worker." A fourth vague category is that of "own-account" (self-employed) workers. What determines whether an enumerator will count a woman who is not in the paid labor force in one or another of those four categories? Rules for enumerators differ from country to country, and are subject to various interpretations even within the same country.

Our problems of interpretation continue when we consider regularly recognized occupations especially in rural areas, where most of the world's population still lives. What determines whether a woman who farms, alone or with a partner, will be listed as a "farmer," "unpaid family worker," or "not economically active homemaker," or "not economically active other"? Again, there are rules, but they are not standard from country to country.

Even in the industrial sector there are enumeration problems. In the third world, how accurately do census takers count the women who are wage laborers in home industries? For that matter, how accurately are the women counted at any work site? Since they are often considered auxiliary labor, in all but the most modern employment settings, women may be substantially undercounted. Women professional and technical workers (a large proportion of whom are teachers) are probably the best counted, and agricultural and own-account workers, most poorly.

A more basic enumeration problem arises from the uncertain capacity of census offices to do systematic counting of any kind, including the counting of births and deaths. Statistical offices are a luxury for poor countries with little governmental infrastructure. Even in the United States, census taking in poverty areas—above all of illegal immigrants—is notoriously unreliable. Sampling techniques can be substituted for complete counts, and frequently are; but these techniques, applied with inadequate knowledge of the total population being sampled from, produce numbers that must be used with great caution.

Finally, even assuming the data are accurate, which they often are not, an obvious question of interpretation remains. Do the categories for which numbers are collected really represent significant indicators of social and economic conditions? Specifically, do they give us significant information about the situation of women with regard to the International Women's Year themes of equality, development and peace? There is a widespread assumption that reporting the proportion of women as compared to men in the labor force and in the school system of a country tells us something about *equality*. But such raw numbers and percentages tell us little about women's opportunities for advancement, about their wages and their working conditions. Similarly, gross national product (GNP) and urbanization—two familiar ways of measuring *development*—tell us little about the resources available to women in different economic sectors, or about the quality of life of the poor. Finally, we hardly know how much *peace* women have, for the impact of war on women and children is not measured as it is for the men who are called into military service. Nor are rape and other crimes of violence against women—a global phenomenon which makes women victims of aggression from within their own communities and even their own families—separately reported on by any national government.

The development of new statistical measures that will tell us more about the quality of life for women as well as men, in relation to equality, development and peace, should be a top agenda item for scholars, and for every UN agency. For the present, however, we must use the categories for which numbers are already collected, and try to take from these numbers what clues we can about the situation of women.

Women's Work

In 1978, one-third of the world's labor force—*as counted by the ILO*—were women. The official figure today would be about the same. If we look at a recent estimate of the percent of women in each of the major occupational categories (see Table 2), we find that women hold half of the world's service jobs, three-eights of the professional and technical jobs, substantial percentages of clerical, sales, farming and production jobs, and even some of the military jobs. Clearly even by the official counts, women are doing a very substantial share of the labor publicly labeled as

Table 2: Women in the world's jobs: occupational categories, by percentage of women in each, worldwide

Occupation	Percentage who are women
Service	50
Professional, Technical	38
Sales	34
Clerical	34
Agriculture and Related Work	22
Production	15
Administrative, Managerial	10
Armed Forces	2

Source: Elise Boulding, *et al, Handbook of International Data on Women* (New York, Halsted Press, 1976).

"work," in addition to their domestic labor which is not counted. The four highest ranking categories of women's employment—service, professional, clerical and sales—belong to the modern sector and are relatively easy to enumerate with ordinary counting procedures. The figures are probably fairly correct. The fifth, agriculture, probably represents severe undercounting because many societies do not acknowledge that the work women do in the fields is "farming." From my own studies I would say that at least half the world's farmers are women, probably more. There are parts of Africa and Asia where women do nearly all the farming, and few areas where women do absolutely no farming.

The *status* of the women in each occupation may be inferred from the fact that only 10 percent of the world's administrators and managers are women. Women, in fact, are concentrated at the bottom rungs of each occupational ladder. In teaching, they are half the world's primary school teachers but only one-third of the world's secondary school teachers and less than 1 percent of college professors and educational administrators. In fact, the reason why women appear so well represented in the world's professional and technical labor force is that primary school teaching is included in the professional-technical category and is considered appropriate work for women, as is the laboratory assistant's role in technical fields.

Since women are at the lower occupational ranks, they earn less than men. Moreover, it has been documented repeatedly that they earn less than men even when doing identical work. The usual rationale for this systematic wage discrimination is that women have husbands who are earning a primary income, and they therefore only need to work for "pin money." Yet a large proportion of women have major financial responsibility for their own households. As Table 3 shows, of the world's women over age 15 at any one time, 38 percent are unpartnered (never married, widowed or divorced). At age 15, in many parts of the world, women both enter the labor force and begin childbearing. Tens of millions of babies are born each year to teenage women—in the first world as well as the third—and many of the

Table 3. The Marital Status of Women over 15, World Averages (percent of all women)

Never Married	23.0
Widowed	11.5
Divorced, Separated	3.5
Total Unpartnered	38.0
Percentage Married	62.0

Source: Elise Boulding, *et al*, *Handbook of International Data on Women* (New York, Halsted Press, 1976).

mothers are single heads of households. Table 4 shows the percent of births to teenage women of selected countries. The United States has one of the highest rates of teenage childbearing among developed countries, but the rates in many developing countries are higher still. The low earnings of women generally, and of teenage women in particular, mean that households headed by teenage mothers almost inevitably become poverty households in which the next generation is reared. This is true in every country, on every continent.

Women in Politics

In most industrialized multiparty democracies, women—despite their success in gaining the vote and in increasing their access to education and jobs—have remained largely absent from the political arena. Hence political strategies for dealing with their continuing economic and social problems have not been easily available.

Some evidence suggests that women's political participation is greater in rapidly developing countries than in those where, as in the Western world, development was spread out over a 200-year period. Table 5 tends to bear out this view. In it we see the representation of women in selected parliaments in 1964, before the major efforts to improve the status of women began, and again in 1975 on the eve of International Women's Year. Each country is also categorized according to the recency of its industrialization, using the "stages of development" as defined by Bruce Russett and his colleagues in the *World Handbook of*

Table 4: Number of births per 1,000 females aged 15–19, per year, in selected countries.

Country	No. of births	Country	No. of births
Japan	4	New Zealand	54
Netherlands	11	Thailand	54
Switzerland	12	Czechoslovakia	56
U.S.S.R.	16	United States	58
West Germany	20	Pakistan	61
Spain	21	East Germany	62
Ireland	23	Rumania	70
Denmark	23	Uruguay	72
Sweden	25	Hungary	75
Belgium	28	Bulgaria	75
France	29	Jordan	78
United Kingdom	32	Turkey	81
Canada	34	Costa Rica	94
Norway	36	Mexico	113
Portugal	37	Cuba	128
Tunisia	39	Congo	136
Australia	41	Togo	147
Israel	44	El Salvador	149
Sri Lanka	50	Chad	162
Italy	51	Gabon	171

Source: UN *Demographic Yearbook 1977*. Figures on developed countries refer to the 1970s; on developing countries, to various years between 1961 and 1975.

Political and Social Indicators. We find that five of the six countries with 10 percent or over of women in parliament are socialist, with the experience of "recent, rapid" development, and four of these five (all but Finland) have one-party political systems. Rapidly developed Japan and Mexico are the exceptions, standing with the majority of "old industrials" in the under-10 percent group, while old-industrial Sweden is the one exception in the over-10 percent group.

It is noteworthy also that all of the high-representation countries except China made further gains in this respect between 1964 and 1975, while all the low-representation ones, except Mexico (a rapid developer with a one-party system), showed very slight gains or losses.

One factor in this difference may be the fact that the more slowly developing countries, even though they experienced many difficulties, political crises and wars, were not faced with the same prolonged and severe social stress, amounting to almost perpetual crisis, that prevailed in the more recently and rapidly industrialized socialist countries and in some countries of the third world, where highly centralized one-party government is the rule. In such conditions women may have been more aware that basic decisions affecting them were being taken in the political arena, and hence have been more strongly motivated to participate in it. Although parliaments in one-party states may not wield the same influence as in multiparty systems, women's participation in them can nonetheless be taken as one index of their political activism generally. By this index, the one-party

Table 5: Percent of women in parliament
and speed of industrialization

Country	Women in Parliament %		Recency of Industrialization
	1964	*1975*	
U.S.S.R.	29	35	recent, rapid
China (PR)	18	14	recent, rapid
Bulgaria	17	19	recent, rapid
Finland	12	22	recent, rapid
Sweden	12	21	"old industrial"
Poland	12	15	recent, rapid
East Germany	7	7	"old industrial"
Mexico	3	8	recent, rapid
Japan	3.5	2	recent, rapid
U.K.	3	4	"old industrial"
United States	2	3	"old industrial"
France	2	2	"old industrial"

Source: 1964 data from Elise Boulding, "The Road to Parliament for Women," presented to International Seminar on the Participation of Women in Public Life, Rome, October 1966. 1975 data from Kathleen Newland, *The Sisterhood of Man*. New York, Norton, 1979.

socialist countries have shown, and continue to show, a much higher degree of participation by women.

A full analysis of women's political participation would draw on many other kinds of data, and might well show that the imbalance is not as great as the single criterion of parliamentary membership suggests. It is possible, for instance, that in the old-industrial countries more increases in participation are taking place at the local level, where they are less visible, than at the national level. In the United States, for example, the percentage of state legislators who are women rose from 3 percent in 1964 to 8 percent in 1975. But other signs are not encouraging. The women who have been heads of government in recent years, while colorful and highly visible, are too few to be typical of the political scene around the world. In one-party states, where decision-making tends to be centered in the party directorate, representation of women at that level tends to be quite low; for example, there are only 9 women among the 288 voting members of the central committee of the Soviet Communist party, and there are no women in the 15-member party Politburo. In general, in all political systems and at all levels of development, it appears that women have made very limited use of political strategies.

6

The Future of Women in the Old World of Power

If there really is a fifth world, a global community of women sharing each other's concerns, then to bring that community to life and make it function for the common good is going to require immense new efforts of understanding and action—especially on the part of the more privileged women of the first world.

We must, to begin with, stretch our minds to encompass these larger realities. What is near looms large to us, and what is far away seems hazy. Women of North America are more apt to pay attention to what is happening to women in our "first world"—in the United States, Canada, maybe Europe—than elsewhere. The women of the third world are not very real to us.

If we do study the world of women as a whole, we are struck by two basic impressions. The first has to do with where most women are. Table 6 shows what a shrinking minority we of the first world are, owing mainly to the higher population growth rates in most developing countries. The developed countries' share of the world's female work force has been declining almost as fast as their share of the world's population. The women's work force in all countries classified as "more developed" was 42

Table 6: WHERE THE WOMEN WORKERS ARE—AND WILL BE
Changing percentages of all women workers, and of world population, between developed and developing regions, 1950–2000

	1950	1975	2000 (projected)
Developed regions:			
Percentage of all women workers	42	36	29
Percentage of world population	*34*	*28*	*21*
Developing regions:			
Percentage of all women workers	58	64	71
Percentage of world population	*66*	*72*	*79*

Sources: For women workers, ILO; for world population, *Statistical Abstract of the United States*, 1978.

percent of the world total in 1950. By 1975 it had fallen to 36 percent, and it is expected to shrink to less than 30 percent by the year 2000. The "less-developed regions" account for all the rest.

The second basic impression is that, as regards the status of women, we of the first world are in most aspects by no means a model for emulation by the rest of the world. To American women especially, this thought may come as something of a shock, for most of us have long thought of the United States as a pacemaker in regard to the status of women, believing that what evolves in American society will eventually spread to the rest of the world. This has, to be sure, tended to be true in education. As Table 7 shows, North America has led the way in conquering illiteracy among both sexes. In Africa and Asia, illiteracy among women exceeds that among men by 20 to 25 percentage points; in North America by only 1 percentage point. The United States is a rich society and can afford to educate its women; but it deserves credit for having done so.

Can the United States also afford to give equal pay for equal work? Apparently not. Is it a model for the rest of the world in this respect? Hardly. Wage differentials and hiring practice differentials based on sex have widened in the very years in which they were supposed to be abolished by "affirmative action" programs. In 1947 the median money income of U.S. female income-recipients over 14 years of age was 46 percent of that of men. (This figure includes nonwage incomes.) By 1970 it had slipped to 36 percent; by 1974, climbed to 37 percent; and 1976, dipped slightly again to 36 percent. In short, American women are substantially worse off now in comparison to their male contemporaries than they were immediately after World War II.

The extent of the difference varies among different job categories. Figure 3 shows women's earnings as a percentage of men's earnings in selected occupations for the years 1956 to 1971. Among sales workers, women earn only about 40 percent of what men earn. Among public school teachers, women get as much as 75 percent of men's earnings. Women professionals generally get about 60 percent as much as their male colleagues. Only for professionals, including teachers, are the gaps between men's and women's wages decreasing. For clerical workers the gap is increasing.

We discussed earlier the plight of women workers, especially

Table 7: Male and female illiteracy rates by continent

	Adult Men %	Adult Women %
Africa	63	83
Arab States	60	85
Asia	37	57
Latin America	20	27
North America	1	2
Europe	2	5
World Total	28	40

Source: Fact sheet issued by the U.S. Committee for UNICEF, 1975.

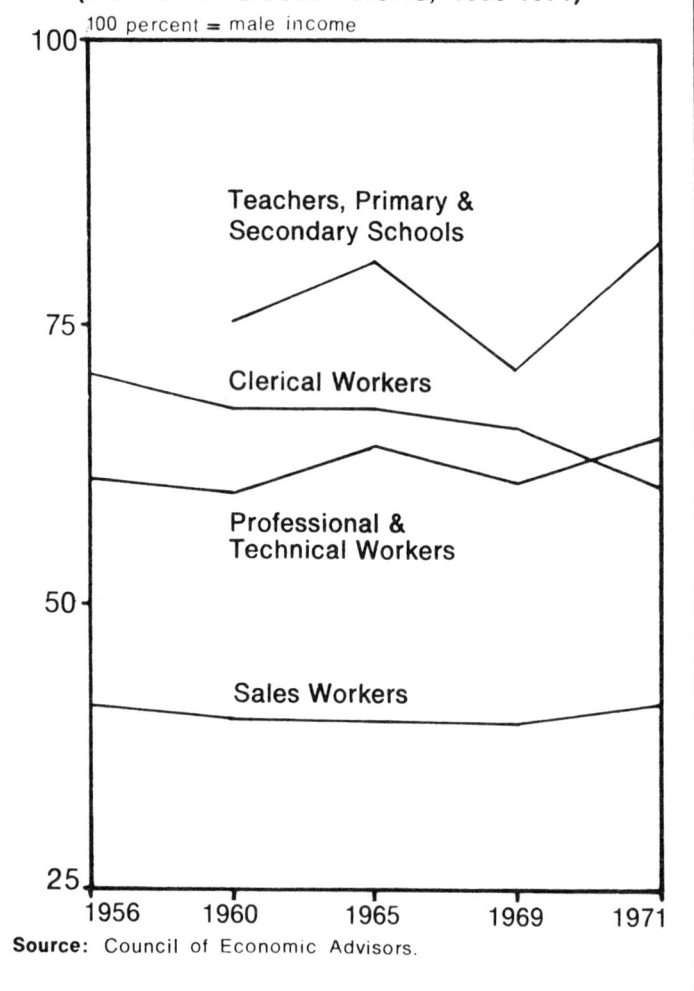

WOMAN'S EARNINGS AS A PERCENT OF MEN'S
(SELECTED OCCUPATIONS, 1956-1971)

100 percent = male income

- Teachers, Primary & Secondary Schools
- Clerical Workers
- Professional & Technical Workers
- Sales Workers

Source: Council of Economic Advisors.

Reprinted with permission from the AFL-CIO *American Federationist* (July 1974), the official monthly magazine of the AFL-CIO.

those in low paying jobs, who are single heads of household. These pay differentials help to explain why 37.3 percent of poverty households in the United States are headed by single women, only 6.4 percent by single men. Evidently there are substantial forces in American society operating on the premise that equalization of wages for women and men cannot be afforded. This hidden premise may have something to do with continuing resistance to the long-pending Equal Rights Amendment to the U.S. Constitution.

Much the same asymmetry in men's and women's wages occurs throughout the industrial world. In 1951 the International Labor Organization sponsored an international Convention on Equal Remuneration, which has since been ratified by 96 countries including all of Western Europe—but not, regrettably, the United States. Even among countries which have ratified it, the disparities which this agreement was designed to end still persist, no less in the old industrialized countries than in those newly industrialized. As recently as 1975, the Council of the European Economic Community felt it necessary to issue an equal-pay-for-equal-work directive, asking the nine member countries to bring their national laws into line with the 1951 convention. Yet wage reports for 1976 and 1977 show the old disparities continuing.

Can the U.S. Help Third-World Women?

The failures to remove economic and social injustice toward women in the United States should not blind us, however, to the fact that American women are in many ways the most privileged women in the world. Suffering from hunger and overwork among women in the United States is minimal compared to the suffering of women in third- and fourth-world countries. The resources that most American women have include time to *think* about what is happening not only to themselves but also to women in the rest of the world—and considerable civic competence to act on that thinking. They also have a government committed, via the Percy Amendment to the Foreign Assistance Act of 1973, to channeling aid to third-world women. Best of all, they have thoughtful and imaginative women's leadership, both in government and outside it, capable of taking action as perceptions of the extent of women's problems continue to grow.

First-world women, as well as their third-world sisters, need to think carefully about the meaning of development and of the integration of women into development. Such words are in general use to describe goals of the women's movement, but they cry out for clearer definition. In one sense, what has already been accomplished in the first world is precisely "development" and the integration of women into it. First-world women are educated in proportions generally approximating the education of men, and they are in the labor force in increasing numbers. Yet, as we see, even in these privileged regions, and particularly in the United States, the dollar earnings of women in all major job categories are far below those of men and the gap in some categories has been getting wider. And a large proportion of these disadvantaged female workers are heads of household in an urban environment seriously lacking in child resources. In such a situation, not only working women but all the people have paid, and continue to pay, a heavy price, especially in the grossly inadequate care and nurture of children. This is not a model of development, or of the integration of women into development, that one would care to commend to other countries.

Then what *is* development? What are we designing when we design "development programs" for the third world? At a very basic level, development means moving away from the stark human need represented by massive unemployment, undernourishment and starvation. Some of the highest human motivations go into designing third-world programs because the situation of the less-industrialized countries is seen to be so desperate. We see severely impacted third-world societies with men dehumanized by want or greed; landless laborers working for a pittance; farmers converting their fields to cash crops sold for export while their families go hungry; migrants from the farms working for a pittance in the cities. We see women working ever longer hours as they must traverse the denuded land over greater distances for firewood and water, and work extra hours in the cash-crop fields

United Nations

Third-world women have their say: two delegates from Senegal leaving a meeting at the World Conference of the International Women's Year, Mexico City, June 1975.

of their spouses or other men, with little time left for tending their own kitchen gardens. They have no time to produce the surpluses that women have traditionally accumulated to pass on to the next generation. Children, bred to be helpers, are often a burden because so many of them die in infancy and many others develop chronic debilitating diseases—thus much of the mother's energy goes into fruitless childbearing.

There is an assumption in the West that this is how it always was in the third world; that only "development" will save those societies, and "integrating the women into development" will save the women. Yet often when data are available on earlier times in specific third-world regions, they suggest that the standard of living and opportunities for women were higher a century or more ago—sometimes as recently as a generation ago—than they are now. Consider this passage from "Women at Work" (an ILO news bulletin, No. 1, 1978):

> It is significant to note that for the first time in the African continent, a shortage of basic food stocks is appearing in countries where earlier there were adequate quantities of food. For example, in the Ivory Coast women have been steadily losing their rights to land for growing food. It was also observed in the river valleys in Upper Volta that women have left the areas in large numbers after settlement schemes were introduced. In West Africa, retail trade which until recently was controlled by women is now steadily losing out to supermarkets and other such establishments.

There is evidence that in the past women and men had types of economic partnership that no longer exist. The women know it from their grandmothers. Perdita Huston writes of this deterioration in her book *Message From the Village* (The Epoch B Foundation, 1978):

> For most of the women I encountered, change—whether seen in their lifetime, or as compared to the lives of their mothers—seems to hold a negative connotation. In their mothers' time, most of them said, "life was not as difficult" or "as complicated." "Now we have to have cash to live." "We have less to eat than before." ... one change mentioned repeatedly and with distress, regardless of country or ethnic or religious identification, was the disintegration of relationships between men and women. Over and over again I was told: "Men were better in the old times; they took care of their families"; "There is no trust between men and women anymore." Older women complained about the lack of communication with their menfolk. Unmarried girls voiced the hope that their husbands would "talk with me," "plan with me," or "be understanding" and spoke of their fear that communication between husband and wife is rare, if not downright impossible.

Women's fear of men may be an old fear in urban societies, where women lost their independent base a very long time ago, but it is a new fear in many rural societies and among new migrants to the cities. High rates of alcoholism among migrant men are one source of fear in their wives; "It's not that he's bad, it's that he got in bad company," the women will say.

Migrant women, whether in third-world cities or industrialized first-world cities of Europe and North America, may be the worst sufferers of all. They have left rural deprivation to experience urban deprivation, and may also lose their husbands in the process. They must then support children in the slums of an alien land whose language they do not know. A few move up to a secure working-class existence. Most do not.

The complex chain of events that reduces individual autonomy in industrializing societies does not, of course, affect women alone. It also affects men who work in large organizations. They suffer from the stratification associated with all large-scale production systems, at least as we have known them in both the capitalist and the socialist modes. And they have to cope with the powerful centralized bureaucracies, agents of military or political authority, which seem to be an unavoidable concomitant of such large-scale productive enterprises—and whose remoteness, arbitrariness and inefficiency have not changed much in 2,000 years. As Henry Jacoby has shown in his book *The Bureaucratization of the World* (University of California Press, 1973), the struggle between central control and local autonomy goes back to the earliest of ancient bureaucracies, and it still continues today.

But if men suffer at the hands of bureaucrats, women suffer more, for bureaucracy has always been a predominantly male world. This fact can be traced to the origin of bureaucratic systems in the authoritarian palace-temple regimes of the earliest city states. Each technological innovation that made new surpluses possible, from plows to irrigation systems to mechanical conveyor systems, was linked to the palace-temple complex. Exclusionary rights to the fruits of the technology were maintained by the military arm of the palace-temple complex.

Technological advance has never stood free of the palace-temple-army complex in any society. Even in an industrial society keyed to the mass market, little has been done to shape technology to the needs of the poor, especially poor women. The stronger drive has been from within the bureaucracy—ever to expand, to improve its tools, to increase its power.

It is one of the clichés of the present era that industrialization has emancipated women by giving them an advanced domestic technology. But little of this technology reaches the poor. And even for those classified as above the poverty level, the system that provides them with such technology is a mixed blessing at best. Against the convenience of electric gadgets, television and frozen foods must be set the heavy cost to millions of mothers of having to pay for these benefits out of wages earned at jobs far from home, and therefore of having to pay also for the child care—often inferior in quality—which they must hire in order to hold the jobs that bring in the wages. On top of all this, women in this predicament must usually accept the lowest-paid work in the job market.

To integrate women on such terms as these into a world economy which spends more than $400 billion yearly on maintaining armed forces would appear to be close to the ultimate in abandonment of autonomy for women. The rehumanization of the world is not likely through such means.

The Responses of Women

What are women to do? To cooperate with those who wish to integrate them into the present international order is to destroy all their hope for a different future. But even the much-heralded "new" international economic order, to the extent that its third-world authors have revealed their intentions, does not promise to be very different from the old—not for the poor, least of all for women. It only offers the opportunity for more third-world women to become marginalized labor in the modern sectors of their national economies, or continue as rural landless laborers (which most of them already are) at slightly higher wages. The bureaucratization of the world will increase, because more centralized planning, on a grander scale than in the past, will be required.

Visible concessions to the needs of the poor will no doubt be included. Special programs under the label "basic needs strategies" will be devised to build small rural factories in which women can work to increase their marginal incomes. Packaged appropriate technologies containing all the recommended small incremental improvements of food storage facilities, wheelbarrows, food dryers, flour mills and high-protein multivitamin food supplements will be sold to women, usually by multinational corporations. Whatever cash surpluses their wage increases might have generated will thus be quickly absorbed in the national or even the world economy.

Ironically, these are all things that women, particularly intellectual women concerned with development, have asked for. (Few people have any idea what village women might ask for.) If third-world women get packaged appropriate technologies from the first world instead of developing the capability to produce their own appropriate technology, we may all be the losers, for the dependency of women may be only further increased.

It is time to learn from third-world women what they want, and to find out what they know how to do already. It is also time for women in the United States, and in the first world generally, to reflect on what we want, what we know already, and what our grandmothers knew. In the third world, when even the most meager resources beyond mere subsistence are available, women generally know how to generate surpluses and to develop credit and insurance systems among themselves. It is this approach, building on existing skills and the tiny surpluses at the bottom rather than on imported resources decided upon from above, that will bring women into development as partners with independent bargaining power and autonomous social goals. The grim alternative is for women to remain as dependents piteously hoping for assistance in mitigating their hardships.

The words de-coupling, de-linking, withdrawal, are often used to describe certain radical third-world strategies for breaking the dependency patterns of the old international economic order. According to this strategy third-world nations will trade with each other and share each other's skills, strengthening their economies by their own resources until they feel strong enough to reenter relationships with more industrialized nations. Oil wealth in the third world has made this strategy less attractive, since oil-rich nations feel strong enough to trade as equals with the first world, and even to invest heavily in the first world—thus denying their investment capital to the less fortunate fourth-world majority, which has not yet shown the courage to de-couple. So the entire developing world, oil-rich and otherwise, has opted for a "new" international economic order which is little but an enlarged version of the old, with continued dependency of the poor countries on the rich.

Women have *not* struck oil. They are poorer, more marginalized than before. Is a de-coupling strategy possible for women? Lysistrata scenarios make good theater but poor social tactics. Women cannot and will not eject the men from their households around the world en masse, with the promise of reentry if they will stop playing war-cum-development games. Furthermore, men don't know how to stop playing such games. That is why disarmament is so difficult in spite of the best knowledge base in history to work with.

Women don't know how to stop the war games either, although the women's peace movement keeps trying. Women do have skills of self-sufficiency, of resourcefulness and inventiveness, of capacity to endure hunger and pain. These are resources that come into play only when there is a perception of the need to draw on them. In the United States and Europe, these skills are going into the establishment of all-women's workshops of all kinds, and all-women's communes where children are reared without violence. Every week the various journals that report the alternative futures movements around the world announce new all-women's enterprises (printing presses, factories, consultant firms), new communes, new networks, new newsletters for women only. The women's self-help health movement, the women's banks, women's cooperatives and credit associations, child care communities, all are essentially movements of strategic separation on behalf of a new future. They are not "anti-male," but rather have a strong task orientation to helping women. For many Western women such movements appear new and threatening. There is a considerable self-consciousness, even hostility concerning them, because they are so unfamiliar.

These movements are not new, however. They belong to the century-old Western tradition of women's self-help organizations initiated by the Women's Christian Temperance Union and the Young Women's Christian Association. The 53 international women's organizations listed in Appendix I range from radical to conservative in political views and social roles, and some may have grown stale in their original purpose, but they do represent a set of autonomous women's voices in the public arena. If they are by and large the voices of privilege, that is neither good nor bad in itself, only a factor to note. They do represent a series of worldwide networks with varying capabilities for autonomous action.

The third world, too, boasts organizations of women for self-help purposes. Those in Africa are possibly the most highly developed. There the traditional women's councils provided the soil that today nurtures the All African Women's Conference, which has a highly developed inter-linkage system with other women's organizations around the world. New associations of third-world professional women are forming to take hold of development thinking for themselves. Three of these in three different regions—the Association of African Women for Research and Development, the Pacific and Asian Women's Forum and the Latin American Association of Women Social Scientists—were independently formed in a single month, December 1977. An Arab Social Science Women's Association was formed in 1979. In each case the intention is to form an independent group of trained women to deal with men, with other women, and with the West, on different aspects of societal development.

7
The Vision of the Future

The motto of the Italian women's movement says *Tutta la nostra vita deve cambiare* (Our whole life must change). But change to what? What do women really want for themselves, their nation, the world? Women have only very recently been asking that question, because they have been so busy adapting to what men want. We get some clues in science fiction written by women. There is an amazing convergence of images of the future by women writers in the direction of a more localist society, using technology in sophisticated but careful ways to ensure humanized societies, interactive, nurturant, nonbureaucratic. Catherine Madsen's delightful story, "Commodore Bork and the Compost (A Homily)" suggests how women would run a spaceship society. It would be ecologically sound, scientifically based, yet informal, spontaneous, warmhearted, and a bit untidy, with lots of room for individualism among its members. The commodore from the tight and tidy male spaceship that visits the women's space ship cannot believe what he sees—most of all, he cannot believe that it *works*.

We know very little about how women would develop and organize technology for human needs because they are rarely in designing or decision-making positions affecting technology. What we need now is a sustained effort by women to reflect, to imagine, to daydream. We need dialogues between rural and urban women, between middle class and working class women, between craftworkers and headworkers, the old and the young, about what "development" might mean for human beings. And we need the knowledge and ideas of third-world women about their own situation and their own needs. How *might* things be, how do the many "we's" of women in different regions visualize the good life for themselves and for the human race? It has been clear since the Mexico City conference during International Women's Year, 1975, that first-world women cannot be voices for third-world women about development. The same truth comes through in recent books giving voice to third-world women of the countryside and of the city, such as Jean Guyot's *Migrant Women Speak* and Perdita Huston's *Message From the Village*. From such sources we are reminded that when women not accustomed to speaking begin to speak, a new social reality becomes visible. In the most unlikely settings, women thus finding their voices can begin to plan jointly how to improve their lives in their own way.

Action for the Future

Our capacity for large-scale social design is limited. We need many economic and social experiments on a small scale, and we need to free women to engage in such experiments. These experiments are and will continue to be carried on both by partnered and unpartnered women. They must build on what women already know how to do, and remove them from the position of being pawns in someone else's development scheme.

What will make this approach different from what women have always done to humanize their lives under difficult conditions? For one thing, the "new international information order" now being debated at the UN may make it different—provided it doesn't become a new pretext for government censorship. Never have social movements had such instant access to each other around the globe. Because many women have, for good reasons, gravitated to journalism and various communication media, there now exists the beginning of a journal-newsletter-radio-TV network of women which can be used to create a multiplier effect for every experiment that is worth sharing. This is one case in which high technology can be put to a worthy use.

The International Feminist Network (IFN) that grew out of the 1978 International Tribunal on Crimes Against Women, and ISIS, the resource and documentation centers set up in Geneva and Rome in 1974 to serve the new international women's movement, are two examples of the many newly functioning networks created since 1970. Other examples include the International Women's Tribune Center, which grew out of the IWY Tribune at the Mexico City conference in 1975; WIN, the Women's International Network (a one-woman operation, unlike the other enterprises); the International Roster of Women Professionals; and the three regional organizations mentioned above. These are not women's organizations in the tradition of the 19th and early 20th centuries. They are all networks, functioning with minimum organization and maximum flexibility.

Moreover, parallel structures now exist in the bureaucratic world. These include national development agencies; no less than 32 UN agencies which have some concern for women in development; and the regional and international UN Research and Training Centers for Women, some recently created and some still in formation. These official bodies will have a challenging time learning to relate to and dialogue with the nonformal women's structures. The older women's nongovernmental organizations may play a mediating role in this process.

What all these developments mean is an end to privatism for women. It is now possible to imagine an autonomous sphere for women that is *public,* from which new forms of economic and political organization can evolve.

In *The Underside of History* I have documented how women over and over again through the centuries have done the invisible work of reconstruction and repair for warring male societies. There may be times coming for the human race when none of the techno-bureaucratic solutions will work. The threat of runaway military disasters, chemical-nuclear pollution disasters, shortages of quickly substitutable alternative energy sources, long-term planet-wide agriculture-impacting climatic changes, and simple administrative overload—all signal an urgent need for local ingenuity, local problem-solving. The ingenuity of women may be the most precious resource the human race has left.

Appendix I
Some Significant Women's International Nongovernmental Organizations

All African Women's Conference
Arab Social Science Women's Association
Association of African Women for Research and Development
Altrusa International, Inc.
European Union of Women
Federation of Asian Women's Associations
Girl's Brigade, International
General Federation of Women's Clubs
International Association of Lyceum Clubs
International Association of Physical Education and Sports for Girls and Women
International Alliance of Women
International Association of Women and Home Page Journalists
International Council of Jewish Women
International Confederation of Midwives
International Council of Nurses
International Council of Social Democratic Women
International Council of Women
International Conference of Women Engineers and Scientists
International Federation of Business and Professional Women
International Federation for Home Economics
International Federation of Mazdaznan Women

International Federation of Women's Hockey Associations
International Federation of Women Lawyers
International Federation of Women in Legal Careers
International Federation of University Women
International Inner Wheel
International Union of Liberal Christian Women
International Union of Women Architects
International Women's Cricket Council
International Women's Tribune Centre, Inc.
Latin American Association of Women Social Scientists
Medical Women's International Association
Northern Nurses Federation
Open Door International
Pacific and Asian Women's Forum
Pan-American Medical Women's Alliance
Pan Pacific and Southeast Asia Women's Association
Soroptimist International
Socialist International Women
St. Joan's International Alliance
World Association of Girl Guides and Girl Scouts
World Association of Women Executives
West European Group of Nurses
World Federation of Methodist Women
Women's International Democratic Federation
Women's International League for Peace and Freedom
Women's International Zionist Organization
World Movement of Mothers
World Union of Catholic Women's Organizations
World Women's Christian Temperance Union
World Young Women's Christian Association
Zonta International

Source: The Yearbook of International Associations. Brussels, The Union of International Associations, 1978. A few recently formed organizations added by the author.

Talking It Over

A Note for Students and Discussion Groups

This pamphlet, like its predecessors in the HEADLINE Series, is published for every serious reader, specialized or not, who takes an interest in the subject. Many of our readers will be in classrooms, seminars or community discussion groups. Particularly with them in mind, we present below some discussion questions—suggested as a starting point only—and references for further reading.

Discussion Questions

The author refers to women as a "fifth world." What meaning does she give to this term, and how does it relate to the first four "worlds" familiar to students of international affairs?

Many failures of economic development in the poor nations, the author believes, are traceable to neglect of the role of women. In your opinion, how should successful development be defined? How does the author's view of development differ from prevailing views in the UN and among third-world governments?

In most societies through most of history, the author finds, women have been subordinated to men and confined to childbearing, child-rearing and homemaking roles. What exceptions can you think of? What can today's industrial societies learn in this respect from other cultures, past or present?

Which do you consider most important in judging the status of women: property ownership? education? access to skilled and professional jobs? equal pay for equal work? the right to vote and hold office? sharing domestic and parental duties with their husbands?

Would you say women are better off in nomadic societies or in the cities of the industrial world?

Why, in the author's view, has the city been particularly unkind to women? How would you solve the problems women encounter in city life, especially in combining their roles as mothers and wage-earners?

The author says that the situation of working mothers with children in American cities "is not a model of development ... that one would care to commend to other countries." Yet the situation of women in developing countries is in many instances far worse, and the "new international economic order" promises little improvement. What approaches to a solution does she offer? Do you agree or disagree with her approach, and why?

Five years into the UN Decade for Women proclaimed in 1975, UN reports found that despite some forward steps, the condition of women in most developing countries is still hampered by a general social prejudice and by indifference among policy-makers. How do you believe such obstacles can be overcome? What role can women of the "first world" play in this process?

READING REFERENCES

Boserup, Ester, *Women's Role in Economic Development*. New York, St. Martin's Press, 1974.

Boulding, Elise, et al., *Handbook of International Data on Women*. New York, Halsted Press, 1976.

Boulding, Elise, *The Underside of History: A View of Women through Time*. Boulder, Colo., Westview Press, 1976.

———, *Women in the Twentieth Century World*. New York, Halsted Press, 1977.

———, "The Road to Parliament for Women," presented to International Seminar on the Participation of Women in Public Life, Rome, October 1966.

———, joint with Patricia Boston Trainer, "Quality of Life, U.S.A.: Costs and Benefits of Urbanization and Industrialization, 1900-1970." Conference Proceedings, Second Annual Session, Institute of Environmental Sciences, Environmental Awareness, San Diego, Calif., April 27, 1971.

Dupire, Marguerite, "The Position of Women in a Pastoral Society" in Paulme, Denise, ed., *Women of Tropical Africa.* Trans. by H. M. Wright. Berkeley, Calif., University of California Press, 1963.

11 Million Teenagers: What Can Be Done About the Epidemic of Adolescent Pregnancies in the United States. New York, The Alan Guttmacher Institute, for Planned Parenthood Federation of America, Inc., 1976.

Friedan, Betty, *The Feminine Mystique.* New York, Norton, 1963.

Guyot, Jean, *et al., Migrant Women Speak: Interviews.* London, Search Press Limited, 1978.

Huston, Perdita, *Message from the Village.* New York, The Epoch B. Foundation, 1978.

International Labour Office, *Woman Power: The World's Female Labour Force in 1975 and the Outlook for 2000.* Geneva, ILO, 1975.

———, "Women at Work," an ILO news bulletin, No. 1, 1978.

Jacobson, Carolyn J., "Women Workers: Profile of a Growing Force." *The American Federationist: The Journal of American Labor,* AFL-CIO, July 1974.

Jacoby, Henry, *The Bureaucratization of the World.* Berkeley, Calif., University of California Press, 1973 (paper).

Newland, Kathleen, *The Sisterhood of Man.* New York, Norton, 1979.

Rihani, May, *Development As If Women Mattered.* Washington, D.C., the Overseas Development Council, 1978.

Russett, Bruce M., Allen, Hayward R., Deutoch, Karl W., Lasswell, Harold, *World Handbook of Political and Social Indicators.* Westport, Ct., Greenwood, 1977. (Reprint of 1964 ed.)

Simons, H. J., *African Women: Their Legal Status in South Africa.* Evanston, Ill., Northwestern University Press, 1968.

Strathern, Marilyn, *Women in Between: Female Roles in a Male World, Mount Hagen, New Guinea.* New York, Academic Press, 1972.

Tinker, Irene, *et al.*, eds., *Women and World Development*. New York, Praeger, 1976.

Wellesley Editorial Committee, *Women and National Development: The Complexities of Change*. Chicago, University of Chicago Press, 1977.

World Plan of Action of the World Conference of the International Women's Year, Mexico City. New York, United Nations, 1975.

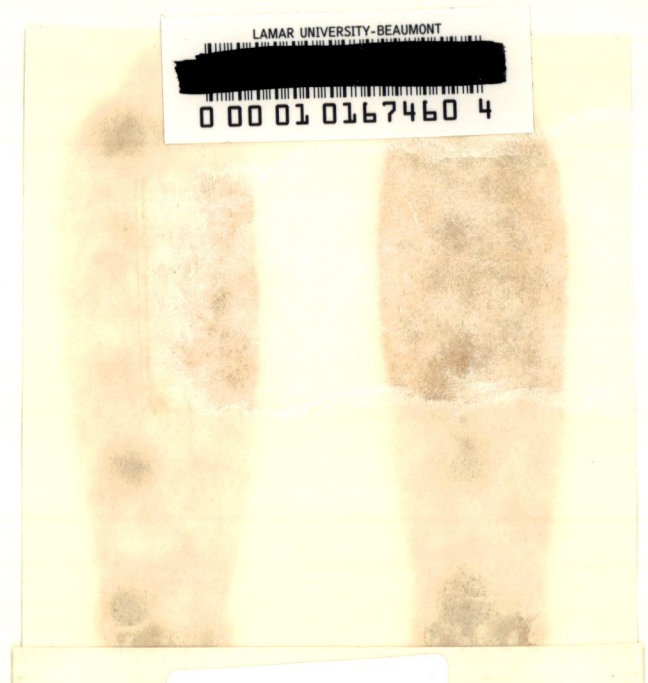